Bumps & Bruises

Heinemann Library
Chicago, Illinois

Angela Royston

Designed by Dave Oakley, Arnos Design
Artwork by Tower Designs UK Ltd
Originated by Dot Gradations Ltd
Printed and bound in China
by South China Printing Company

08 07 06 05 04
10 9 8 7 6 5 4 3 2 1

**Library of Congress
Cataloging-in-Publication Data**
Royston, Angela.
   It's not catching bumps and bruises / Angela
Royston.
      v. cm.
Includes bibliographical references and index.
Contents: What are bumps and bruises? -- Who
gets bumps and bruises? -- Falls -- Bangs --
Trapped fingers -- Bangs on the head -- Inside a
bump -- Inside a bruise -- Serious head injuries --
Treating bumps and bruises -- Getting better --
Preventing bumps and bruises -- Protecting
your head. ISBN 1-4034-4823-X (hbk.)
   1. Wounds and injuries--Juvenile literature. 2.
Head--Wounds and injuries--Juvenile literature. 3.
Bruises--Juvenile literature. [1. Wounds and
injuries. 2. Head--Wounds and injuries. 3. Bruises.]
I. Title: Bumps and bruises. II. Title. RD96.15.R696
2004
   617.1'3--dc22
                              2003019815

Acknowledgments
The author and publishers are grateful to the
following for permission to reproduce copyright
material: pp. 4, 18 SPL/Dr P Marazzi; pp. 5, 10, 15,
19, 22, 23, 24, 27, 28, 25 Trevor Clifford; p. 6
Mark Harwell Stone; p. 7 Taxi/Carl Schneider; p. 8
The Image Bank/Ben & Esther Mitchell; p. 9
Taxi/Steven Simpson; p. 11 Getty Images/Stone/
Nick Dolding; p. 13 SPL/Oscar Burriel; p. 17 SPL;
p. 20 Phillip James Photography; p. 21 Last
Resort; p. 26 Masterfile/Rommel; p. 26
Powerstock; p. 29 Getty Imagebank.

Cover photograph reproduced with permission of
Trevor Clifford.

The publishers would like to thank David Wright
for his assistance in the preparation of this book.

Every effort has been made to contact copyright
holders of any material reproduced in this book.
Any omissions will be rectified in subsequent
printings if notice is given to the publisher.

Contents

Some words are shown in bold, **like this.** You can find out what they mean by looking in the glossary.

What Are Bumps and Bruises?

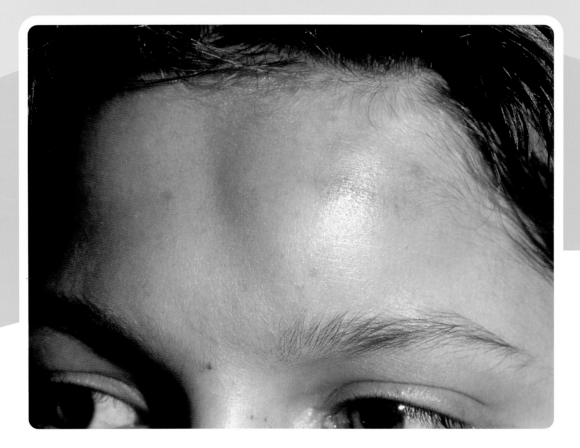

When your skin is hit or banged, it may form a **bump** or a **bruise.** A bump is a hard lump that forms over the part that was hurt.

A bruise takes longer to show on the skin. At first the skin may turn red. Then the bruise appears later as a blue or black mark.

Who Gets Bumps and Bruises?

Anyone who falls or is hit hard will probably get a **bump** or a **bruise.** Children and older people are most likely to fall.

People who play sports, such as football, soccer, or baseball, are also likely to get bruises from time to time. You cannot catch a bump or bruise from someone else.

Falls

You can sometimes fall when you trip over something, or when you lose your **balance.**

The faster you are moving when you fall, the more likely you are to **injure** yourself. The harder the fall, the bigger the **bump** or **bruise.**

Bangs

You might bang yourself when you bump into something, or when something hits your body. For example, you might bump into a table when reaching for something underneath it. Most bangs and bumps are **accidental.**

People should not hit each other on purpose because they can get hurt. Boxers use gloves to soften their punches.

Trapped Fingers

Children sometimes get their fingers trapped in a drawer or a door. Do not hold the edge of a door or a door frame. Your fingers can get caught if someone shuts the door.

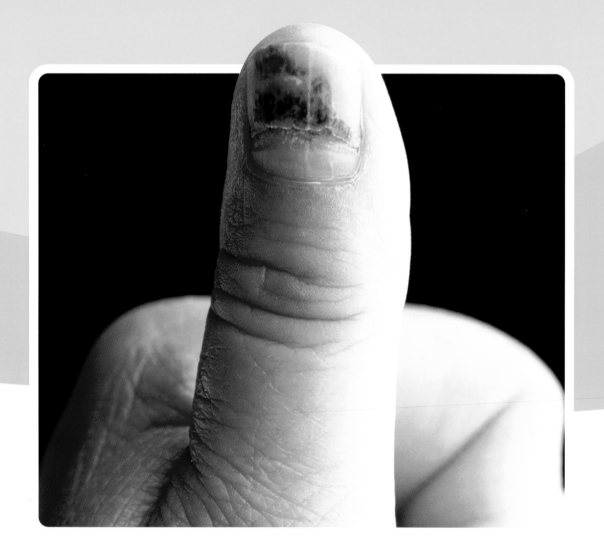

If your fingers are trapped, your fingernails may become **bruised** and turn black. If the base of the nail is damaged, the whole nail may fall off.

Inside a Bump

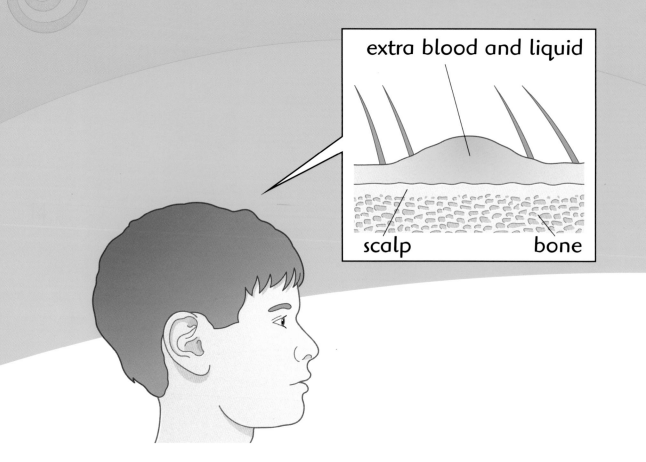

extra blood and liquid

scalp

bone

A **bump** is made of **swollen** skin, blood, and other liquid made by the body. A bump feels hard and hurts when you touch it.

Your body forms a bump to protect the **injury** while it heals. The extra blood in the bump helps the injury to heal. As the injury heals, the bump gets smaller.

Inside a Bruise

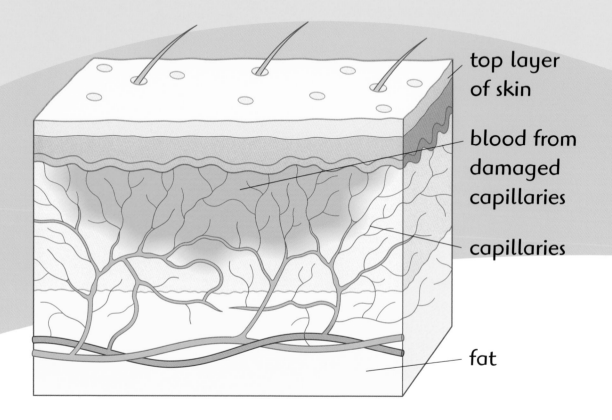

top layer
of skin

blood from
damaged
capillaries

capillaries

fat

Your skin is fed by tiny tubes of blood called
capillaries. Each tube is as narrow as a single
hair. When your skin is banged, some of the
tubes burst. This causes a **bruise.**

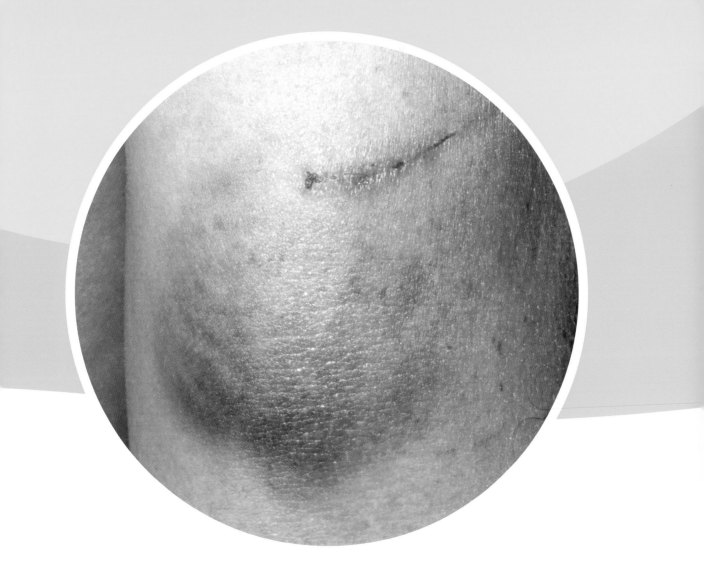

The blood leaks into the **flesh** around the
bang. As the spilled blood dies, it turns black.
You see the spilled blood as a bruise through
your skin.

Bangs on the Head

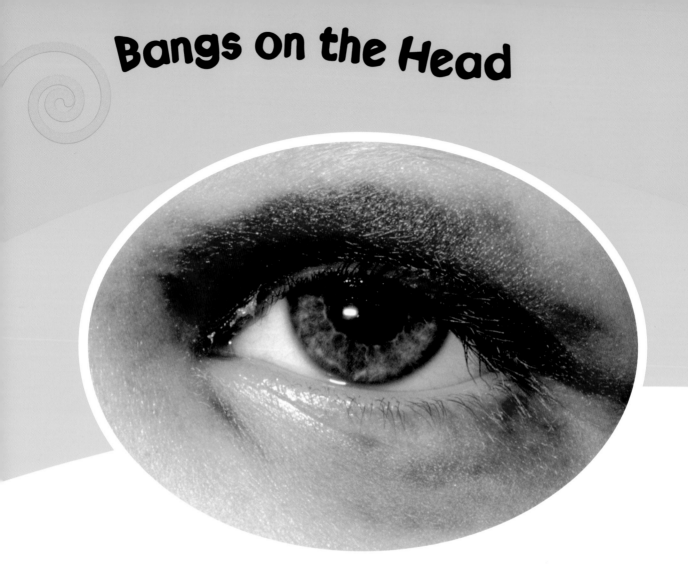

Your head and face can easily become **bruised.** You do not have much fat or **muscle** between the bones and the skin to **cushion** any **bumps** and bangs.

Head **injuries** can be dangerous because your head includes your **brain,** eyes, ears, nose, and mouth. A hard hit on the head can cause a bad injury.

Serious Head Injuries

If your head is hit hard, you may **injure** your **brain.** This is called a concussion. It can make you feel confused. You may even become **unconscious** for a time.

If you think you may have concussion, an adult should take you to the hospital or to see a doctor. A nurse or doctor will check your **injury.**

Treating Bumps and Bruises

Bumps and **bruises** heal themselves. You can help to reduce the **swelling** in a bump by holding an **ice pack** on the **injury.**

You need to keep the ice pack in place for several minutes. One way to make an ice pack is to wrap a package of frozen peas in a towel.

Getting Better

As a **bump** heals, it slowly gets smaller. As a **bruise** heals, it stops hurting and changes color. It changes from black to purple, then to green, and then to yellow.

24

The bruise changes color as the dead blood is slowly cleared away by fresh blood. Bumps and bruises all eventually go away.

Preventing Bumps and Bruises

You can wear special pads on your knees and elbows when you skateboard or in-line skate. They will **cushion** you if you fall.

People who play sports wear protective clothes, too. Soccer players wear shin guards under their socks to protect their legs from **bumps** and **bruises.**

27

Protect Your Head

You must be extra careful to keep your head safe. Always wear a **helmet** when you ride a bicycle. The helmet **cushions** your head if you have an **accident.**

Falling off a horse can easily **injure** your head, too. If you ride a horse, you should always wear a riding helmet.

Glossary

accident   something that happens by mistake

balance   being able to stay in one position without falling over

brain   body part that controls the rest of your body

bruise   blue or black mark on the skin that is caused by a bang

bump   hard lump that forms over a part of the body when it is injured

cushion   soften the effect of a fall or hit

flesh   soft muscles and fat that cover your bones

helmet   hard, strong hat that protects your head. It is important to wear a helmet that fits well and is not damaged.

ice pack   plastic bag with frozen contents used to make swelling go away

injure   hurt or damage

injury   bump, bruise, cut, or break that hurts or damages the body

muscle   part of the body that moves the bones or flesh

swelling   when part of the body becomes bigger. The swelling is caused by extra fluid under the skin.

swollen   become bigger

unconscious   not awake

More Books to Read

Gordon, Sharon. *Bruises.* New York: Scholastic Library Publishing, 2002.

Royston, Angela. *Why Do Bruises Change Color?: And Other Questions About Blood.* Chicago: Heinemann Library, 2003.

Royston, Angela. *Safety First.* Chicago: Heinemann Library, 2000.

Index